Table Of Contents

DEDICATION:

This book would not have been possible but for the love and support of my wife Melanie, daughter Tricia, and son Tony.

Also, no writer writes alone. There are those trusted few who encourage the freedom of expression that words bring, those who challenge us to see the opportunities, to try new ideas, and those who inspire the creative dream. Anna D. Banks, Marta Colon, Bob Miller and Bert Shockley, Thank you. For without your help, patience, and guidance, this work would not have been possible.

RULES THAT DESCRIBE OUR REACTIONS TO TECHNOLOGIES:

Anything that is in the world when you're born is normal & ordinary & is just a natural part of the way the world works.

Anything that's invented between when you're 15 & 35 is new & exciting & revolutionary & you can probably get a career in it.

Anything invented after you're 35 is against the natural order of things.

Douglas Adams, Author

PIECES OF THE PUZZLE

H ello and welcome to Pieces of the Puzzle. You picked this up, looking for a new idea to figure out what to do now. Since you're ready to put together a plan to manage your career, you need to take a look at the different pieces of the puzzle and study the big picture.

GETTING THE PIECES TO FIT :

Job search is very much like putting together the pieces of a puzzle. This is something that our parents taught us. Our early toys were all about puzzles, putting the blocks together in a tower that wouldn't fall, dressing a doll, or putting the shapes in the right hole. To get our search off the ground, you first need to identify what career fits your skills and interests, call all your friends and family to ask if they know anyone who is hiring, build a resume (focusing on those skills and the achievements that we bring, notice it said skills, not baggage), write a cover letter that excites an employer to turn the page to read the resume, identify and practice the interview questions that we know are coming, create a thank you letter that says more than just thanks, contact our references to let them know we're looking and to ask if they will give you a good reference, and make sure that you have clothes that fit for the job you're interviewing for.

FINDING THE MISSING PIECES:

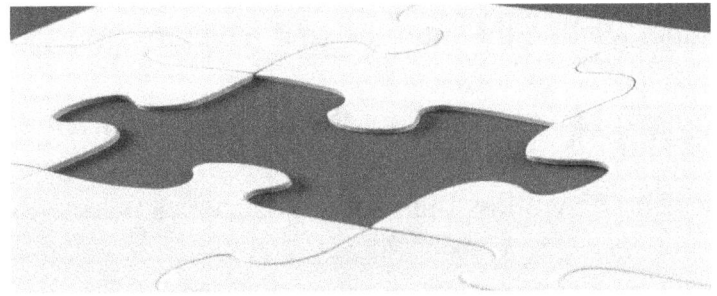

Sometimes the piece fell on the floor, is stuck in the box, is covered by another piece, but when we look with eyes that see, we find it. It's the same with looking for a job. We have to look all over to find what we really want to do. Network, call those friends and family. People want to help, but you have to ask. This is the old saying, "give a man a fish, feed him for a day; teach a man to fish, feed him for life." The people you know can help you learn by supplying you with the bait, job leads, because they know someone, who knows someone, who knows someone, that has an opening at their fishing hole.

But don't put all your eggs in one basket. You have to spread out the pieces to find where they fit. So surf's up dude. Get on the internet, find the companies you want to work for and learn about them. Read the what's new section as well as the products\services pages; this will let you know about any changes that are happening, such as a new products\services, building, and opportunities. Also, go to the job sites that specialize in the careers you want and register. It's free, and it works!

Newspapers still have want ads. The Sunday paper contains the most ads, and Wednesday is the next most popular day for companies to advertise. The rest of the week just repeats these ads. But the business section always has articles about what companies are doing, new products, services, buildings, etc., which can give you ideas on where to look for employment.

Walk and or drive around and look. Everyday there are trucks driving supplies and services. Commercial and residential buildings are going up left and right. Stores are always opening. Opportunity is there for you.

RECHECK THE PICTURE ON THE BOX:

Trying to put a piece of the blue sky in the blue ocean, no matter how hard you try, isn't gonna work. Take the time to look at the picture for other clues as to where the piece goes. The same goes for your job search. Expand your search. Look for other ways to apply your skills, instead of just searching for job titles.

For example, non-profit companies are great places for people with various skills, looking for meaningful work. You're a teacher's aide but want to go into the medical field. See which skills (caring for others, record keeping, and communication) cross-over. Focus on where you're going, what you're doing to get there.

EXPERIMENT:

Twist the piece. Find other pieces that fit, that make a little scene in the middle instead of as the main picture. Putting together a puzzle takes time and patience. So be willing to try different things. Get out of your comfort zone.

✢ Make the cold calls and the follow up calls. Write a script or a few notes to help guide you through the call. Practice first, make a few trial calls to friends to become used to talking on the phone for a purpose. If you know what you're going to say ahead of time, you can make your calls work for you.

✤ Research the company and their competition. The better you know the industry, the better you can explain to an interviewer not only how you can do the job better, but the why's behind the companies goals.

✤ READ! Read, read, and read. If you want to do something else, if you want to do more, and take in new ideas, reading lets you do it at your pace, in your own time.

FINALLY, THE BIG PICTURE:

The last piece fits. The picture looks great and you're happy. You finished what you started, the pieces came together. You did it! Now before you pack up the puzzle and put it away, remember what you did to finish it. Use the job skills you bring and learn new ones to compliment them. Know how your skills transferred and how to make them stronger. You are willing and able to learn, so be ready to prove it. Bring that to work with you. Not only will you find a place that fits, it will give you a place to challenge and inspire you to find the solutions to

the puzzles at work.

What Am I Going To Do Now?

T he rumors are for once true and after devoting time and energy into a career at company X, when the layoffs hit, your name was on the list. First comes that sinking feeling of what am I going to do now. Then, as you're walking out to the car with a box of desk stuff, you realize that tomorrow is a sleep late day, go sign up with unemployment, and the desire to "take some time to catch up on some stuff."

Or, are you a recent graduate, taking your first steps into the adult world of the 40 to 50 hour week? Are you full of energy and ideas, looking for a path to the "promised" career.

Are you re-entering the work force? Have you been a stay home parent who now wants\has\needs to get up off your best intentions and rejoin the army of the employed?

The fact is most of us will be unemployed at some point in our lifetime. According to government statistics, we will have 15 different jobs in several different careers. And it takes longer to find work, about 90 to 180 days. So the question remains, what to do?

Relax and don't panic. It's not the end of the world, even though it feels like it. Because we identify our sense of self with our job, the loss of employment affects us hard. But, what has happened is that on the journey of life, we get to take a new path. Here are some suggestions to make the trip go smoothly.

WHAT ELSE CAN I DO

With all of the opportunities out there and the skills (transferable, technical, job specific) you possess, deciding on what you want to do can be confusing. To find out if moving into a new field is right, you need to have accurate information. One extremely cost efficient way is to take an on-line assessment. Career sites, like ***gettinghired.com*** or ***careerplanner.com***, offer workplace skills assessment to see if the new career path that you want to follow will lead to success. Plus, this will give you leads and insights into other fields where your skills can be used.

And since these are job sites you can post your resume and see various job listings. This is a productive way for you to learn more about yourself and have employers find you based on what skills you can bring to the table.

We've all heard, "it's not what you know, it's who you know." And in the current job market, those words ring with an unmistakable truth. Now is not the time to throw a pity party and cut yourself off from the rest of the

world. It **IS** the time to work your network.

Contact everyone you know; family, friends, former colleagues, ex-supervisors, anyone you know. Call these people and ask them the magic questions; are you hiring? And don't forget the equally important follow up, do you know anybody who is hiring. Remember, you don't know who the people in your network know. A name, a lead, anything you get from a personal source is worth more than answering an ad. The company looking to fill a position will be more willing to take a chance on someone who was recommended than just off the street.

WHAT TO DO, WHAT TO DO

When you sit down and begin to create your notes for your resume, look at your accomplishments first. The duties and responsibilities of a job are the routine tasks. What you want to do is look at what you did; promotions, awards, raises, certificates earned. And you want to quantify it. Think like an employer when you write down what you did. If you think like an interviewer, you will know what they want to hear. Don't just say "I was a cashier", instead try, "accurately handled over $2,000.00 in sales transactions while providing attentive customer service to over 100 customers." You could also say "can provide attentive Customer Service, by resolving the customer's situation in a fast paced environment, with a smile." The second and third answers give the reader information on the quality of your work.

PUNCH THE CLOCK EVERYDAY

You have to handle your career search as seriously as a job. Get up everyday, write out a daily schedule to follow and follow it! Write out specific weekly goals that are measurable and take action. Make those follow up calls, network, read the business section of the newspaper, ask questions, and do your research. Research the job market, opportunities, companies you want to work for, trends and patterns. Read anything current you can find that has information on the career you want to enter. The better informed you are, the better decisions you can make concerning your future.

Looking for a new career is not the end of the world. Instead, it's an opportunity to learn and grow. And by doing the little things, the light at the end of the tunnel won't be an incoming train, but a clear path for a more rewarding and fulfilling career.

Who Do You Know?

REASONS WHY YOUR NETWORK IS IMPORTANT

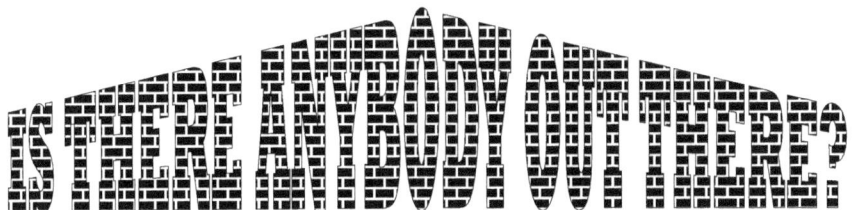

Pink Floyd, The Wall

When we're looking for the right career opportunity, we think of ourselves as alone. As if no one has ever had to do this before. Some of us see the path to success glimmering in the sunshine.

DO YOU KNOW ANYBODY HIRING

Reach out and touch someone, anyone you know. Your friends, family, former co-workers, classmates, your kid's friends parents, their teachers, people who work in the store you shop at, is an excellent start of your list of contacts. The easiest way to get your foot in the door of a company is by someone opening the door for you. This is what a person in your network can do for you and why it is so important to stay in contact with people.

Remember one reason why you're doing this. You don't know who these people know, who they talk to on a regular basis. And while the company they work for might not be hiring at the present time, someone they know may know someone who knows a company that is hiring.

And people like to help others. But they don't know if you need any help unless you ask for it. So make up a list of your contacts, go over it twice. And make those calls.

ENCOURAGEMENT, DIRECTION, SOMEONE TO BOUNCE IDEAS OFF

Who do you know, who can become a mentor? Somebody you respect, who has handled adversity and has not only grown but thrived as a result. Who do you know that owns their own business? Here is a problem solver who can recognize an opportunity and create a way to profit from it.

When they asked Aristotle Onassis, who was the richest man in the world at the time, what would he do if he lost everything, he had a great answer. He said he would take any job he could to survive, save his money, buy a suit, and take the richest man in town out to lunch. His reason was that the "crumbs from a rich man's table is worth more than a banquet with a beggar." Successful people have more resources, such as contacts, who are decision makers, business owners, all of whom could be on the lookout for a new employee.

Find someone who you trust, who believes in your talents and abilities. They can provide focus, help you plan the next step, and push you out of your comfort zone. They can help you rehearse your answers to the interview questions. It's your journey, but everybody needs someone to lean on for guidance and strength. Who is yours?

PUTTING IN A GOOD WORD

Once you know the career path that you want to go down, the next step is to come up with references that can help you. The best references are people in the industry that you want to be a part of, in positions of authority. They can speak about your intangible qualities, the skills you possess, and the type of person that you are. Former supervisors are an excellent reference since they can give a first hand account of you as an employee and talk about the quality of your work. Co-workers can talk of your team spirit and your problem solving and\or training abilities. There are many other people you can put down as references like your teachers, friends, and even your pastor.

When creating a reference list, the following information is imperative:

Person's Full Name (no cute nicknames)

Job Title

Name of Company they work for

Address (either one, home or office)

City, State Zip Code (that matches the above address)

Phone Number

E-mail address (if they have one)

Here are a few additional notes to help make your references meaningful. ***Ask them first***. These are some of the first people you contacted when you started looking for work. This lets them know that you value their opinion. Make sure that the contact information is accurate and that they are employed. You are known by the people who you know, so an employed reference will reflect better for you. Give your references a copy of your resume, this way they have an idea of what skills and achievements you want them to talk about. If you want them to talk about why you're perfect for the job, make sure the message stays consistent.

"Is there anybody out there?" Yes, if you know who to ask and what they can do to help. So you have no reason not to make a list, pick up the phone, and invite

someone to lunch to talk. See where the trail of

breadcrumbs leads.

Writing Your Resume

D o you have a resume?

This question is all that one hears today when looking for a job. But what is a resume? It is a marketing tool that you use to describe your life-work experience. It should show your background, skills, work experience, and accomplishments, and how they were used to help you succeed.

Here are a few tips for getting your resume read and acted upon:

1. No more resume objective section, use a summary of skills instead. All objectives sound the same, "I'm looking for challenging and rewarding work as a (place job title here) for a company that's growing,

with an opportunity for advancement." When everybody says the same thing, nothing stands out. Instead, use a Skills section where you can describe 5 or 6 reasons to hire you for the position you seek. This will provide a common theme to all your correspondence, show effective communication skills and focus. It will also help with answers to common interview questions such as "why should I hire you" or "what can you do for this company that the others can't" or "what are your strengths" or "tell me about yourself." A well written summary enables you to focus your answers and let your future employer know why you are the best candidate.

2. Watch the little things. Include your name, address, up-to-date phone number and professional e-mail address. Use a simple font. Print it on white paper.

Make sure the copier you use makes a good copy. Know your dates of employment, the months and year. Watch your spelling. Again, WATCH YOUR SPELLING! It has to be legible, that means clear, precise and to the point. It doesn't matter what it looks like but if there are mistakes, missing information, and careless errors, then your resume is likely to end up in the circular file. Look at it this way, would you want to pay someone who makes careless mistakes when being in charge of telling their own story? I think not.

3. 2 pages are ok **IF** you have the experience to back it up. Face it, in today's job market; we'll have 7 different careers and about 15 different jobs before we retire. Think about it, do you have 10 years experience or 1 years experience 10 times? When you have similar jobs, the duties and responsibilities

are the same. But if you grow in your career, you can talk instead about what you learned and how you build upon the previous experience to make an impact with each new employer. To cut that experience down to a page doesn't tell enough about you, just make sure the most important information is on the first page. And if you're going for your first job, talk about what your school or community(volunteer efforts) achievements were.

4. Have someone else proof read it when it's finished. To us, it could look like the Mona Lisa, to others, a finger painting. Get the opinion of one you respect and listen to what they say, the importance of having a mentor in your network.

5. Do: use action works and key industry phrases (this is one area where your research will pay off); use bullets to emphasize points; list any awards,

certificates, licenses, degrees; list volunteer experience (especially when you have no employment history). Remember the acronym KISS-Keep it short and sweet.

6. **DON'T**:

- ✤ use personal pronouns

- ✤ include personal information (marital status, kids, social security number, religion, height, weight)

- ✤ include a photo

- ✤ put your references on the resume

- ✤ mess with academic credentials

- ✤ change dates of employment or list just years

- ✤ repeat the same job tasks over and over, instead talk about what you accomplished

✤ list hobbies\interests unless for example, you're a skier looking for work as a ski instructor

The idea is to craft a professional, focused message about what you bring to the table.

7. It's not chiseled in stone. Always be ready to tweak your resume by adding new skills, new jobs, and new certificates or licenses or degrees. When you answer an ad, they always list the skills the position requires, make sure that they are listed in your skills and qualifications section.

The goal is to create a document that gets read and gets results. One size does not fit all; you should have different resumes that play to your various skills and achievements for each opportunity you are going to pursue. The resume won't get you hired, but it will get you in front of the

people who can.

Key Word Games

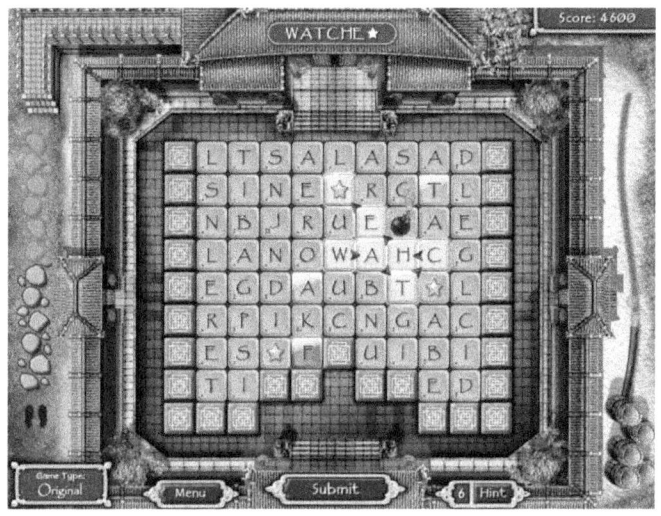

"Why don't they do what they say, say what you mean, one thing leads to another"-The Fixx?

We've all heard the expression choose your words carefully and in writing your resume, the right words can mean the difference between a great resume, making a positive impression or an ineffective one, that gets no results. It's all about marketing yourself, by using your communication skills to get your message read. Let us look at how we can strengthen what we want people to learn about us.

CHOOSE ACTION WORDS

Select words that fit your mouth. And know the meaning of the words you use. When choosing words, look at the deeper meaning and which fits better. Use power words, words that describe action. People constantly say they are reliable and dependable. But what they really mean is responsible. Here are a few examples: create vs. develop, flexible vs. versatile, assist vs. part of a team.

Watch out for wishy-washy statements such as assisted. 'Assisted' brings the image of someone who stood around in the background and only did something when someone told them what to do.

On the internet, you can find lists of words to use and ones to avoid. Research shows that you are paying attention to recent trends and patterns. You did the work, get the proper credit.

USE AD WORDS

In the Ad that you answered, the company told you exactly what they were looking for. So why don't you tell them exactly what they want to hear? To get what you want, an opportunity, you need to tell them, in the words they chose to hear, why you are the best candidate.

When you answer an Ad, your resume is placed into the company database. Once here, it is scanned by a computer program, looking for Keywords. Which words? The words used in the Ad, of course! The ones with the highest number of matches are then selected, by the

44

computer, to go to the next step. This is a prime example of why you should tell the company what they want to hear. Sending a resume electronically, a person does not read it, a computer does. Mail your information, make a person open the letter and read the contents. Be an individual who stands out and gets things accomplished.

KNOW THE INDUSTRY

This is one area where your knowledge and research about your career choice does matter. By using the "language" of the industry, you can make your points meaningful. It shows interest in the field and respect for the job/company. The more you know, the better you can stand out and make an impact. This is especially true for entry level positions. You are used to doing research in school; now use that skill to find out what the industry is all about and what potential employers are looking for.

When you say what you mean, with words that fit, people notice. And since success in your career depends on your communication skills, make sure you choose the right words.

Sample Resume

Your Name
Street Address
City, State Zip Code
Phone Number
E-Mail Address

SKILLS:

✤ Using bulleted text, list your six most

important skills

✤ Talk about accomplishments

✤ The skills written here will help you answer

the common interview questions such as:

➢ Why should I hire you

➢ What are your strengths

➢ Tell me about yourself

➢ What can you do for us that the

other candidates can't

This will help you to focus your message during the interview and help you stand out

EXPERIENCE:

Month\year started, left   **Name of Company**   City, State

Job Title

- ✤ Talk about your accomplishments, what you did and how you did it
- ✤ Mention numbers; money handling skills, number of students, patients, clients, customers, meals you served, *size matters*!

EDUCATION:

Month\year started, left   **Name of School**   City, State

Degree\Certificate\License

earned

Here is an excellent place to talk about the clubs you were involved in, any academic awards, classes you took and excelled at, anything that has a bearing on your skills and abilities.

Now it's your turn. Start to write out your skills,

achievements, and abilities. This is your chance to

practice what you've been reading about and give it

meaning, to you.

Skills

Experience

___/___ to ___/___   _____   _____
mm yy   mm yy   Name of Company   City, State

_____
Job Title

Job Responsibilities/Accomplishments

_____

_____

_____

_____

_____

_____

___/___ to ___/___   _____   _____
mm yy   mm yy   Name of Company   City, State

_____
Job Title

Job Responsibilities/Accomplishments

_____

_____

_____

_____

_____

_____

____/____ to ____/____   _____   _____
mm   yy   mm   yy   Name of Company   City, State

                                _____
                                Job Title

                    Job Responsibilities/Accomplishments

                    _____

                    _____

                    _____

                    _____

                    _____

                    _____

Education

____/____ to ____/____   _____   _____
mm   yy   mm   yy   Name of School   City, State

                                _____
                                Degree/Diploma/Certificate

____/____ to ____/____   _____   _____
mm   yy   mm   yy   Name of School   City, State

                                _____
                                Degree/Diploma/Certificate

Getting Results From A Cover Letter

"YOU NEVER GET A SECOND CHANCE TO MAKE A FIRST IMPRESSION"

Before the advent of computers and the subsequent security measures undertaken by employers due to 9-11, job seekers had an easier time. You got dressed for success (men a suit and tie, women a dress or pants suit), walked into a company you wanted to work for and got an application from Human Resources (formally Personnel). If they had time, hands were extended and shaken. If you made the right impression, you were brought into an office where questions were asked about what you bring to the table. An interview on the spot was not uncommon in days past.

Or, a parent, relative, or family friend would bring you to work to "meet" the boss. After an exchange of pleasantries and a few simple questions (like how do you know so and so), you started work the next Monday.

But today, things are different. In the earlier cases, your appearance, interests, or relationships opened doors. Now, you need a professional introduction to the company, a way for them to see who you are, what you know, where you learned it, and how you use what you know. It is time to utilize your communication skills and market your abilities. A well written cover letter has one purpose and one purpose only, to get a potential employer to turn the page and read the resume. It will not get you a job; it will not get you an interview. It will wet the company's appetite to want to learn more about you.

An internet search for cover letters will lend itself to over 1,000,000 different results and offers, ranging from boiler plate (something to avoid as recruiters recognize them easily as they look pretty and say nothing), to creative, to having one written for you for a fee ($ 29.95 per letter, with a free re-write if you don't get results within 90 days). Writing the letter doesn't take a master's degree in English. As long as a few points are kept in mind during the process, your letter will be great.

✚ Always include a cover letter anytime you send out a resume, whether by e-mail, fax or mail.

✤ You want it focused to the job you are seeking. When you write about your skills, make sure they are ones valued in the field you want to join

✤ Write the letter to a specific person. This is where your research will pay off. A letter that starts off To Whom It May Concern or Dear Sir\Madam, might be correct, but is cold and impersonal. With the emphasis placed on building professional relationships, you need to know the person's name and job title that is screening the applicants. Make sure you get the name and title right or the letter and résumé goes into the circular file.

✤ Want a way to stand out in a positive way? Write the letter to the president of the company you are looking to join. The letter that comes down from the top will get more action than the one coming in the same door as every other applicant. When the boss hands it to the right person, your cover letter and resume WILL BE read. It's marketing, getting your message out.

✤ KISS –Keep It Short and Sweet. The idea is to get them to read your resume, not to show off your creative writing skills (unless the job calls for Creative Writing).

✤ Spelling and grammar ARE MORE IMPORTANT than formatting. Nobody will care what the letter looks like if it's filled with careless mistakes that could have been avoided.

- Past accomplishments = future success. Talk about the results that you've achieved, not so much the process. People want to hire winners, put yourself in that spotlight.

- Use action words and be positive.

- Only include salary information if it's specifically requested.

- ASK for an interview.

This leads us to look at the hows of a cover letter. This document should be 3 to 4 paragraphs in length. Brevity; get to the point, make the point, is the key to effectiveness. And don't be afraid to use bullet points to emphasize key points.

Paragraph 1: List the job you're interested in and how you learned about the opportunity

Paragraph 2: This is the one called, "You seek, I have".

Your research will pay off here. You can talk about your specific skills and experiences that you have and relate it to the opening available. Don't go overboard; KISS is crucial at this juncture.

Paragraph 3: State your interest in the job opening, your availability for an interview and specifically ask for an opportunity to sit down, face to face. They can't see the sincerity in your eyes or hear it in your voice from a piece of paper.

If you don't hear from them within a week, send a letter again. In this letter, you can mention other transferable skills and how they fit the position that is open. Be persistent and consistent; in any office, papers are misplaced or not read when things are hopping. By sending it again, it will double the chances of somebody reading it. And follow up with a phone call, as this shows

that you're a go-getter, who is interested. If you do what

others won't, you'll get the results they don't!

Solving The Interview Puzzle

"Can you come in for an interview", the voice on the phone asked? "We have an opening at 2:30pm on Thursday."

All that hard work paid off. You were effectively able to market your skills in such a way that the employer saw the value of your achievements and accomplishments. Now the fun begins, solving the interview puzzle. Once you have the steps in place, you can then make your plan of action. Follow it carefully be ready for the unexpected and watch the puzzle picture become clear.

PREPARATION IS THE KEY

Research, research, research. Know the company and spend a few extra minutes reading up on the industry and competition. And it's easy to do, since all you need is a computer and the right search engine. Just type in the name of the company and voila, instant information; go to the ABOUT US page and look for WHAT'S NEW page. This will give you the company history, tell you about what the company feels is important, and more importantly, some idea of their future plans. Also, go to the career or job page and read the job requirements and make notes of which ones you have. These will become your talking points.

Next, go back to the search engine and read up on the industry. This information will be somewhat general; trends, patterns, opportunities and if you look hard enough, salary guidelines.

If your skills do not include computers, your research shall have to be in the library. Here you can find recent newspapers and magazines which will have the information you are searching for. Locating books about the industry, with the aide of a friendly librarian, has the advantage to teaching you about what you did not know.

Another resource is found in the school you were\are attending. The guidance department, for you in high school, or the Career Placement office at your college or university can put you in touch with people who can answer your questions. They can teach you about the industry or even a specific company, alerting you to positive growth and opportunities that is not yet public knowledge.

Answering Interview Questions

Next to meeting your significant other's family, the most challenging, stressful opportunity we face to impress others, is when we interview for a new career position. Nervousness is a by product of how well prepared we are. When we're ready for it, the interview lets us bring our marketing material to life. You know the questions that are going to be asked. So write down the answers. Edit them down, and ask yourself "if I was hiring someone for this position, is that the answer I want to hear?" And practice them again, till you are confident in the answers. The more you practice, the better you will do when the door opens and you walk in and sit down, ready to go.

Here is where the summary approach pays off for you. It helps you focus on your message and deliver it consistently. The summary helps you to answer the following common interview questions:

- ✤ Tell me about yourself?

- ✤ Why should we hire you?

- ✤ What do you bring to the table?

- ✤ What can you do for us that the other candidates can't?

- ✤ What are your strengths?

Your well written summary has opened the door. It helps you to talk about your skills and how you use them to successfully complete projects. You can deliver a message with confidence, has value and meaning to a potential employer. How well you prepare FOR the interview is directly proportionally to how well you'll do IN the interview.

Another group of questions deal with your work relationship and examples of these are:

- ✤ Describe your last boss
- ✤ What did you like/dislike about your last boss?
- ✤ How did you get along with your co-worker, customer, and supervisor?

What are they really asking when you get these questions? They are asking about your judgment and personality. The interviewer is looking to see if you can follow directions, your work ethic, your ability to get along with others, and your conflict resolution skills. As much fun as it may be, it is NOT the opportunity to trash others. When you do, the message heard is "I make no mistakes", "I'm never wrong", "I'm a Diva", and "I'm smarter than anyone else" in an arrogant way.

Other pieces of the interview puzzle to keep in the corner of your mind are:

- ✤ Keep everything positive.
- ✤ Do not use yes/no answers. They close conversations and reveal very little about your skills and abilities.
- ✤ Make sure you hear the question and answer the question that is asked. Do not volunteer any information that could make you look unfit or questionable. Be honest, tell the truth. Explain the positives, what you learned

about the results of your previous actions before you tell them what happened. You want the positive heard not lost since they stopped listening when you went down the path of negativity.

- Tell your story; you are the one who has to make sure <u>your</u> story is told.
- Tell the truth and take responsibility for what occurred. A favorite saying is, "It is what it is, deal with it and move on".
- When answering, think like an owner. Telling a story about your prowess in the arts or sports (unless it is RELEVANT to the job by showing the lessons learned from overcoming obstacles as a team) has no value to an employer's bottom line.

✤ Sell your professional benefits, features and skills. State their value and potential positive impact.

✤ When talking about challenges, look at this as an opportunity to discuss what you learned and how you grew from the experience.

✤ And most importantly of all; hear the question, understand the question and answer the question.

Interview Questions

Here is a list of some of the most popular interview questions. Use the space below to write out your answers. And then practice!

Tell me about yourself

What do you bring to the table?

What are your strengths?

What can you do for us that the other candidates can't?

Why do you want to work here?

Why did you leave your last job?

What are your goals?

Where do you see yourself in 5 years?

Tell me about the worst boss you ever had.

How would you solve the following problem?

What do you know about our company?

What accomplishment in your past job stands out?

What are your weaknesses?

What did you like best about your last job?

Describe how you can resolve a conflict between (co-workers, a customer, a supervisor).

Questions You Ask

A common question as an interview is winding down and the employer wants to find out about you is "Do you have any questions?" This is an excellent opportunity to find out about the position and the company. Even though an interview should be a conversation, this is your time to sit back and listen to the answers, as your future choices may well affected by what is said.

Answering *NO* to this question could close the window of opportunity. Employers may feel you are not interested in the job, are lazy and did not do any research, is arrogant or just not interesting.

By asking thoughtful questions, you will be able to stand out and complete another piece of the puzzle in your career search. The questions you ask will show the potential of the position in terms of future growth and about the "corporate culture". You want to make sure you choose a place where you feel comfortable, where you want to go everyday and make a difference.

When it's your turn, try these questions to find the answers you seek.

- What would be the first project that I would be assigned to work on?
- What do you like best about working here?

✚ Could you tell me where the people who have

held this position are today?

✚ What qualities are you looking for in the

person for this job?

✚ What skills are valued in employees who

move up in the company?

✚ May I contact you if I have any additional

questions?

Dress For Success

"'CAUSE EVERY GIRL'S CRAZY FOR A SHARP DRESSED MAN" ZZ TOP

Getting dressed is one of those simple things Mom taught us growing up. Make sure your socks match, your underwear is clean, that your pants fit AROUND your waist – not below it, and wear a jacket or you'll catch cold. Right, that's our basic fashion lesson, the rest comes down to choice. So how do you choose to be thought of; serious about finding the right career or is what you have on say "I don't care".

Have you ever sat there and saw that the interviewer was dressed nice compared to what you had on? And remember how that feeling made us lose focus. Here are a few tips and tricks to feel comfortable. Dress for the industry; if it is very corporate like banking and finance, a formal look is the one you seek. If you are looking retail; a shirt and tie for men, a nice dress or pair of slacks with a blouse will do. One last note, when dressing for an interview, remember to dress for the job you aspire to.

WOMEN:

Let's start from the bottom up. A simple pair of black shoes, heel not too high, will be fine. You can wear either a pair of slacks or a skirt. This is an interview, not a night out at the club so; the skirt should be at least finger tip length.

A blouse not cut too low or revealing with a scarf or nice looking necklace, dress it up a bit more with a vest or jacket to round out the ensemble. Make-up is used to enhance, not as camouflage in the corporate battlefield, or to use another old saying "less is more". The same should be said about perfume, you don't want someone to smell you coming. Hair should be neat and natural for you.

We're not out to fling the bling, so no more than 3 bracelets, two or three rings is fine, and earrings should be on the small side. Piercing, while cool, also creeps people out, just a friendly tip. And you should remember that if you have tattoos, make sure they are covered.

This is not a night out clubbin' with your friends; you are a serious professional with skills and talents that the interview will showcase. Make sure you dress the part.

MEN:

This will be short and sweet. Shoes and socks, black, pants either black or blue that fit, a belt that's for more than show, shirt, button down the front with a collar, the bare minimum of what you should be wearing. Yes, there are exceptions, like a tie, jacket, or the standard suit if that is the style of dress. But guys, seriously, do you want the job? If so, this is the basic look, classic and standard.

Watch the bling, the cologne should not cause the interviewers eyes to water, hair neat and trimmed. Same suggestions as far as piercing, tattoos, earrings work here as well.

Opening The Door of Opportunity

Wake up an extra 15 minutes early, call this ***just in case*** time, for anything that can come up. You **DO NOT WANT** to show up **LATE**, I repeat,

DO NOT SHOW UP

LATE! If something should come up, call.

Prove that you value their time by showing common courtesy and reschedule.

Now, I know that dollars are always a concern, but if you want to be taken seriously as a professional, look the part. Buy a folding pocket folder with a pad that has the interview contact information, your questions, and extra copies of your resume, certificates, and list of references. Be prepared for success and it will soon follow.

As you walk out the door, put on the most important piece of the puzzle in talking to people. Your smile ☺,

use it all day long. Get your face used to wearing one. A smile lets the world see that you are a happy person and *that* is the type of person other people want to be around. And while we're here, mind your manners, sit up straight, a firm handshake, and look the interviewer in the eye (while juggling a bowling ball, an apple, and an egg – just kidding!).

Walk in the room confident in your abilities and in what skills you have to offer. This is where the fun begins. Consider the interview like a blind date with a preacher's son\daughter, at the church picnic. You are dressed nicely, ready to be a good listener. You are there to talk, to find out information. It's a "getting to know you, getting to know all about you" time. And if they like you and what you say, there are more "dates" in your future.

When hiring new employees, people want to bring into the company likeable people. If you're all up tight, you will come across as being unsure or that something is being hidden. Employers want to hire responsible, honest, team members. This is the image you want to exude. Know who you are professionally and what skills you have to offer. Go and deliver your marketing message with confidence.

Keep your answers positive. Tell the truth, stick to your message and make sure to look at the questions from a business' point of view. If you can figure out the why behind the question, you can focus your answer better. No one knows what you can bring to the table better than you. You're ready.

FOLLOW THROUGH WITH YOUR FOLLOW-UP

Think about how the interview went. Which questions did you answer easily? And which ones need practice? Look at everything that went right. After that, plan out how to improve what didn't. You know you can do better.

A strong last impression helps to seal the deal. Continue reading to learn more about this point.

The How & Whys of Saying Thanks

"We have a few more interviews scheduled and we're looking at making a decision toward the end of next week. Thank you for coming in and talking to us." Those words are the last words we hear when leaving an interview. We get up, shake hands, extend a few cordial words, and walk out the door. Now, all that's left is the waiting game, right?

WRONG.

There is still something left to do, a critically important piece to the job search puzzle that needs to be filled in, the "Thank You Letter."

Don't underestimate its power, as most candidates do. It could be a deciding factor in your favor, especially when other candidates with similar experience, qualifications and skills are awaiting their turn to dazzle a prospective employer. And most employers expect candidates to write a Thank You Letter. And since you want to stand out, make sure your letter is an effective one.

PURPOSES OF A THANK YOU LETTER

This letter is your last, best chance to have an one-on-one conversation with your future employer. Many people use a form letter, which sounds "nice" but says little. Do not use a form letter; write a personal letter to each person you spoke to during the interview. This is known as attention to detail and will, once again, enable you to demonstrate another skill you have.

There are three ways a focused letter can help you as long as you know what your purpose is.

#1: You know you're perfect for the job. This is a one-on-one opportunity, your last, best chance to talk about you, to reinforce your good points. Plus, it shows you are courteous, knowledgeable and professional.

#2: You misspoke or were unclear about some of the answers you gave. You have a chance to correct and explain what you really meant to say in a more relaxed forum.

#3: You were not asked about other experiences and skills you have that will enable to successfully fulfill the requirements for the position. Here is where you can talk about those skills and how they will let you make an immediate, positive, productive impact.

#4: Other opportunities may be available in the future better suited to your talents and abilities.

Regardless of how you decide to send your Thank You letter, follow professional business letter standard. Since e-mail is the quickest way, more candidates are utilizing this method. But using the cutesy NET stuff, like emoticons, short hand and acronyms, are not the way to go. A Thank You card or hand written note are also acceptable, especially in fields where dealing with people, are key parts of the job.

As with any letter that has your name on it, by you,, make sure spelling (especially names), titles, grammar are all correct. All of this will help you to be remembered in a positive way.

If you do what others won't, you'll get the results they don't.

Sample Thank You Letter

Your Name
Street Address
City, State Zip Code
Phone Number
E-Mail Address

Date

Person's Name

Title

Company Name

Street Address

City, State

Good Morning,

Thank you very much for taking time out of your
busy day to talk with me about the ***[job title]*** opportunity.
(Talk about why you wanted to work there. What was

your impression of the company, say why you found it positive)

Judging by our discussion earlier today, I believe that my qualifications are an excellent fit, particularly my *[specific education, experience, skills, etc.].* The position is exactly what I'm looking for, and I'm confident that I can be a significant contributor to the continued success of *[company or department name].* I sincerely hope you agree.

Thanks again for interviewing me. If you have questions or concerns, please feel free to contact me. I look forward to hearing from you again.

Sincerely,

Your Name

Working A Career Fair

Personal contact, the face to face meeting, is the best way to introduce yourself to a perspective employer. Even though there are more ways than ever to get your marketing message out, career fairs let employers see the look in your eye and the confidence in your tone. This piece of the puzzle can become your interview if you're ready, willing and able to take on the challenges.

Career Fairs work for you when you know how to work them. It is a place where you can use your communication skills to stand out. And all those "toys" on the table, pick them up on your way out! Remember, you are there to market yourself, interviews happen on the spot, be ready for anything.

✝ Relax; you're going to do great today!

✝ Look over the list of who's going to be there and pick out your top 10! Do some research about the companies who'll be there. If you know about any new products or services that the company is providing, it will help you stand out. Better to talk to the ones you're really interested in after you work out the nervousness by practicing with a few companies that are not high on your list.

✝ Before you go in, make sure that you have plenty of copies of your resume and a pad and pen to take notes. Be prepared to write down who you spoke to and what you talked about; make sure you get their business card to get the correct spelling of their name, title, and company. When you write your follow-up letter, it will help them remember you.

✤ Be ready for those pesky interview questions. You know they're coming, so practice your answers.

✤ Dress for success. When you look good, you feel good and that confidence will show! You want to look like a professional.

Once you're inside:

✤ Take and read any material on the table before you talk to someone. This will give you time to do additional research and to help you get any last minute hints.

✤ Listen to the conversation to the person in front of you. You'll hear the same questions and it will give you time to make your answers better.

✤ Shake hands and talk to the person

✤ Ask for an application if one is not offered.

✤ Ask the right questions. Prepare your top 5 and be sure to practice them. Try to ask a question like "what made you choose to work for this company and why do you stay?" This type of question will tell you about the corporate culture and future opportunities.

✤ Make sure you get the business cards of the people you talk to.

✤ Do what the others won't. Send a follow up letter and a copy of your resume by the Friday after the fair, so it arrives first thing Monday morning. They saw over 100 people. Do something positively professional to stand out and get your resume read.

✚ Be prepared to follow-up with a call on the Wednesday after the fair. To get the job you want, you have to be consistent and persistent!

Job Fair Questions

You only have a few minutes to make a memorable impression. Have a few, good questions ready to ask and also as important, what not to ask. Here are a few examples of both.

Questions To Ask:

1. What kind of skills and experience do you look for in the employees you hire?

2. How long does the hiring process take? What does it consist of?

3. What advise would you give to someone starting in this field?

4. How did you get involved with this company?

5. What's the one thing that most surprised you about this company?

6. What kind of positions is your company looking to fill in the next 6 months?

Questions Not To Ask:

1. How much does the position pay?

2. Is tattoo removal covered under the health benefits?

3. What does your company do?

4. Would anybody notice if I came in late and left early?

5. Do you provide lunch and snacks?

6. Where does the department spend beer o'clock?

I Got The Job, Now What Do I Do?

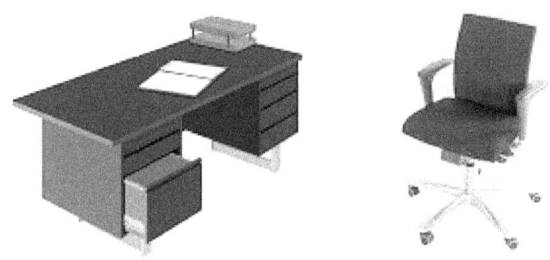

O k, you wrote the resume, mailed the cover letter, answered the questions at the interview, sent the thank you letter, received an offer, negotiated, and finally accepted the position, so the hard work is over, right?

In fact, the hard work has just begun. This is the chance you worked for, where your time and effort paid off. At first, any new opportunity can be a bit overwhelming; Rome wasn't build in a day, so listen and observe what's going on. Get the lay of the land and see how the pieces of this work place puzzle come together to form a picture. See your piece and do your best, that's all anyone can expect of you.

✤ *Bring energy, enthusiasm and a smile with you to work every day*. During the interview, you said you were interested, could learn, and smiled. You wanted to be there and more importantly, were able to show it. Keep that lesson in mind. Just showing up isn't enough.

🏵 ***Common Sense, the most uncommon sense***

of all. It's almost funny, if it wasn't such a

problem. People walking around, cell phone

glued to their ear, talking about their personal,

private, and in some cases, intimate business

in graphic detail. Trying to walk into an

elevator before letting the riders out or fishing

off the company pier (looking for love in the

office, during business hours) is another

example of the lack of common sense.

Coming to work and "sharing" the flu with

your co-workers. Telling people to check you

out on youtube.com, after a weekend

adventure. These are a few of the times

where thinking before you act will save your

professional reputation.

- ***Seek new duties***. The best way to grow in a company is to look for opportunities to try new things. Training programs, those in-house or with tuition reimbursement, pay for themselves in a number of ways that can affect your bottom line.

- ***If you use the phrase, "it's not my job", soon it won't be.*** Everything that affects the company you work for, affects you. Companies want employees who show a willingness to do whatever it takes. So before you say it's not my job, try to help. If you have to get someone else to help solve the situation, stay and learn in case this particular problem comes up again. This will show a

willingness to learn and someone who is
responsible.

✤ *Use your Communication Skills.* Don't wait
for people to come up and introduce
themselves; walk up and say hello. Ask
questions and LISTEN to the answers.
Making a few new work friends will make
coming to work more enjoyable and help get
you into the "team." And these co-workers
are those whom you can ask for help.

✤ *Mistakes Happen.* Over eagerness, lack of
information, wrong information, poor
execution, lack of funds, no support, are some
of the reasons why the project was less than
successful. While it will seem therapeutic,
blaming others can give you a terminal career

injury. Bottom line, fixing the problem is the most important item on your to do list. When these career bumps come up, admit your part and learn from it. By taking responsibility, you can earn a second chance by being honest. Pointing fingers solves nothing and can hurt a team's productivity. Plus, you may need the help of those who you threw under the bus on a future project.

✤ *Etiquette and Net-iquette are important.* Saying hello, thank you, and please to everybody, shows you care and are interested in others. This is the type of person others want to be around. We learned these basic rules of manners a long time ago and they are still being taught by parents today.

Net-iquette is etiquette for the internet. This is a tool that you use to make your work flow. It should not be used to visit dating sites, e-bay, or to instant message your sweetheart. Plus, most companies do keep a record of all internet traffic. Big brother does know who you are, where you've been and what you're doing. If you have any question about the appropriateness of the web sites you're visiting, ask yourself if you'd want your daughter to visit the site.

✤ *Doing your Holiday Shopping in the Company Supply Cabinet.* Here again, common sense should tell you that if you need a bottle of White Out or a pad to do your job, go get it. But if your child is making the world's largest paper clip chain, make sure that if didn't come out of the company closet. Every dollar that is spent in replacing supplies that are misappropriated is one less dollar to go to raises.

✤ *Personal Calls on company time.* Just because you use a cell phone to make your personal calls doesn't mean that this is no longer a problem. You are paid to work, not to make sure when Aunt Emma is turning 75 and you need to talk about what to get her. That's your personal business and it should be handled on YOUR time. The cell phone is a wonderful invention, use it on breaks to reach out and touch someone.

❖ ***Know when to start looking for the next opportunity.*** To be truthful, this starts on your first day. You should always be on the lookout for ways to grow and develop your talents and the companies' bottom line. However, if your job performance is not getting better, if you are having problems getting along with others, if the organization is no longer the type in which you can contribute or grow professionally, if you develop unprofessional habits, before you are asked to leave, get your resume ready and contact your network.

❖ ***Manage Your Career.*** Create a plan of action to keep moving forward. There were many changes that you made to get you to this point. Remember what you did positively, and repeat these experiences. It is your career, you are responsible for it moving forward. You can make it happen.

You were happy when you got the job. Now, let's make sure you're doing everything necessary to keep it.

Value of Volunteering

"IT TAKES A VILLAGE TO RAISE A CHILD", AFRICAN PROVERB

"DO YOU HAVE ANY EXPERIENCE?"

It seems that every employment ad today is looking for experience in that particular line of employment. The problem is, how can you acquire experience if no one will offer you the right opportunity.

A great way to gain that practical career knowledge and experience is to volunteer. Training programs are great ways to build a foundation of information, but experience is the best teacher. This is a great way to grow and expand a network. People you meet in this way will respect what you do. They will respect your dedication, passion, and commitment to a cause. They will see you as a hard worker and a contributor.

You can volunteer at your child's school as class parent (organizing, purchasing, communication, record keeping), at a hospital (caring, concern for others), shelter, soup kitchen, library, museum, first aid squad, fire house, police station, your place of worship, the recreation department.

This shows a person who uses time wisely and it gives you the opportunity to learn the job from the inside.

GAIN KNOWLEDGE AND EXPERIENCE

Textbooks, classrooms and the internet are great places to learn the theories, the why's of a job. But the how's of the position come from actually doing. This is where theory meets reality. Here is where you can hone your skills and make a difference while learning. You will have the opportunity to see what your chosen field is like on a day in, day out basis and talk to people as they are doing what they are doing. You'll be able to pick up the jargon (the language) of the industry so you know what people are saying. The major benefit is when you sit down to interview, by speaking "their language" correctly, you stand out.

COVER GAPS

One way to fill in a resume is with education. This is a great way to show that one has the willingness and ability to learn. But here again, learning is theory; If everything is perfect, this is what should, could, and will happen. As we know, life isn't perfect and that's where volunteering comes in.

Not only does it take abstract learning and make it real, it provides the opportunity for hands-on experience. It covers gaps and can be listed in chronological order in the resume under experience, instead of buried at the bottom, which is common on most resumes. Volunteering shows drive and desire to work or help benefit others. It shows hard work, it shows that you aren't a lazy couch potato waiting for your shows to come on. It talks about what you value and that you are willing to do for others.

SENSE OF SELF-WORTH

Sometimes when you're unemployed (or under employed, a growing phenomenon), you don't feel good about yourself. Volunteering, helping others is a great way to counteract those feelings of inadequacy. By giving back, you can share your most precious resource (Time) and gifts (talents) with people who need. An increased sense of self, knowledge, practical work experience, giving back to others, these are just a few benefits to sharing your time with others.

The Training Piece of the Puzzle

E very time a puzzle is completed, it becomes a piece in a bigger puzzle of who we are. To make a career move, having the skills and knowledge necessary to succeed, is imperative. Experience, gotten by volunteering, interning, or on the job, is an excellent teacher.

There are a variety of certificates and state licenses you can earn or prepare for in training classes. Ideally, you want to make sure the classes taken lead to a recognized credential. You have to jump through a few extra hoops to earn them, but it's worth it. The certificates you receive from a school or learning center, unless it is accredited by the state, is only a glorified certificate of attendance.

As for why you want certificates, licenses or credentials, and should have one, here are a few reasons.

- ✤ This will give you an edge in the job market and enable you to stand out from the crowd
- ✤ Shows future employers that you invest in yourself
- ✤ It proves you have the knowledge, skills, and abilities needed to not only survive but thrive in the right career opportunity. It's one thing

to say that you're a problem solver, it's another to have proof

🍀 It provides the first step on a career path and makes it easier for a person to advance since they have the skills necessary to grow and develop.

🍀 It can help to identify which skills could be stronger.

And don't worry if you got your license in NJ and have moved to Ohio. Most states will accept credentials from other states; it's usually a matter of filling out forms and paying a fee.

A Lesson In Time

T ime is the great equalizer. There are only 24 hours in a day and no one can buy more time, it can only be spent. Some want to control time, but no matter how much you might beg or plead, it is the same for everyone, rich or poor, the great equalizer.

Time is also a resource that can be managed and maximized. Keep in mind the following ideas, when looking at how to make time work for you.

FINISH ONE THING FIRST:

Even though multitasking is the latest buzz, when juggling tasks, sometimes we forget about keeping our eyes on all the balls in the air. And when they do fall, the time spent doing damage control wasn't worth the trade. Juggle what you can, but finish what needs to be finished first. By doing so, you will find a little oasis of sanity and calm, and are better able to move on to the next task.

FLEXIBILITY:

Being organized and completing tasks actually helps you to be flexible. As you have more flexibility in your schedule, you find that you have more opportunities to do what has to be done. And this flexibility lets you build beneficial work relationships since you can now talk to and help your co-workers. Once they see that you are willing to be a part of a team, it's easier to ask for and get assistance when you need it.

GET ORGANIZED:

Busy people write things down. It gives them a map to follow, a direction in which to go. This is a HUGE timesaver since it helps you to work smarter, not harder, under pressure. Write stuff down where it's supposed to be written. All those sticky notes with names and numbers should go into your phone book. Date and time notes should be written in your calendar. Deal with each piece of paper once; read it, then file it, pass it on or can it. This way your focus is on results, not being busy looking for stuff.

DAILY GOALS:

Spend a few minutes before leaving for the day writing out the next day's to do list so you can hit the ground running. This will help you to look at the time available and how best to plan your day. It's easier to get things done, when you know what you have to do. You'll remember to carry out the important tasks first and to not major on the minor. Gather the information and materials you need for the project before you start. This will help your production and stay focused on what you're doing.

TAKE TIME FOR TIME:

The one advantage that smokers in an office have is that they have to get away from their desk to enjoy a cigarette. This gives them the opportunity to relax and develop an idea. It's an opportunity to talk to others and brainstorm. Now if you don't smoke, walk outside and get a breath of fresh air. Let nature help recharge your battery.

Also, if a colleague walks up to talk while you're working

on a deadline, schedule a time to talk to them later on in

the day. By getting away from your desk, the surge of

ideas increases as the blood flows.

DO THINGS RIGHT THE FIRST TIME:

Carpenters have a standard rule, measure twice, cut

once. The idea is to double check what you're doing

before executing. This will cut down on costly mistakes

and make you more productive in the long run. Nothing

wastes more time than having to do a job over and over

again. Look for ways to cut out repetitive tasks. Learn

from your mistakes. By doing things right the first time,

you'll have more time.

The bottom line is this, have a plan in place to help you manage time. This will enable you to be productive instead of looking busy.

Solving The Puzzle: Why You Need Goals

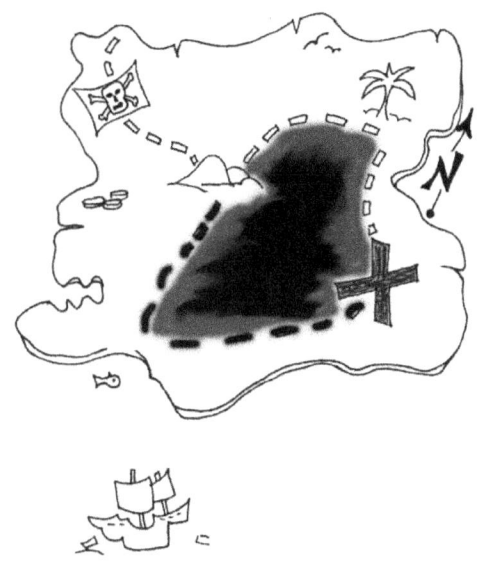

"CAN'T GET TO WHERE YOU WANT TO GO WITHOUT A MAP." SID

Where are you going? What are you going to do with yourself? What do you want to be when you grow up?

Where do you want to live? What do you want to drive?

Do you have a picture of it in your mind? Do you have it

on a piece of paper with a date that you'll have? Do you have a plan? Or is what you have a dream? Want to make your dreams come true, write them down and work your plan. The magic word is goals; here's how they work.

WHERE DO YOU WANT TO GO

You need to know exactly what you want, be specific. Right now, you're looking for the right career opportunity. That's the long term goal. What are you going to do to achieve this goal? Here are a few suggestions of what is meant by specific goals.

+ Contact 5 to 10 people everyday when actively looking, per week when employed where we want to be, doing what we want to do, to keep your network current.

- Fill out 5 to 10 job applications everyday. Go to the job web sites and register with each and every one.

- Research what education, experience, knowledge, and skills are needed in the career field you have chosen, so you can focus your message.

- Find a social group where business people look to expand their contact list. Usually, this sort of club will meet for breakfast or after hours. Remember, you're there to make contacts, not to stuff your face or get tanked.

- Keep a record of everything you do, each e-mail you send, each business card you receive. This is your record of accomplishment, so when you're getting frustrated, you have a tangible record of all your hard work, which is your motivation to get up and go. A successful person gets up one more time and tries again.

These are just a few examples. Add to the list, go ahead, and be creative. This is your plan, where do you see yourself. What can you do to get there? Write it down, roll up your sleeves, and get to it!

WHY YOU NEED A PLAN

This will help to create the best way to go forward. It gives you a bulls-eye to aim for. Plus when you make measurable goals, you can manage the process, you are in charge. These goals have to be able to grow and change, depending on how it's working. Looking for a job is as hard as working at one, with one major difference; you are the boss with the product to market.

HOW WILL YOU GET THERE

You wrote the plan, execute it! Write your list and put it someplace where you can see it everyday. Look over your results to find out what's working and work that. Don't go fishing in a pond that is empty of fish, i.e.: since your job search is broke, fix it. Be creative, look for new ways to get better results, like making follow-up and cold calls. When you can look at the big picture, you can see the forest through the trees and find the path that works for you. It's up to you to manage your career, be ready then opportunity knocks.

THE NEXT LIST

Just because we've accomplished one goal or one set of goals doesn't mean you're done. Time to write out the next list, the same way you attacked the first.

✤ Read 15 Minutes a Day – We change

everyday. By the new information we hear

and see everyday, a new message is heard.

Some of what we hear is positive, some not

so. But with reading, we choose the message

we want to experience. This is something you

do for you. It can help you to relax, to learn,

to be exposed to new ideas. It could give you

new insight as to some of the mysteries of

life, can make you laugh, make you cry, help

you find out.

✤ Learning is for Life – One way to grow, to

change and develop, is to learn something that

we did not know. We can take up a class at

the local high school, look at the bulletin

boards to see if there are any clubs meeting, any lectures, something that will get us out of the house and interacting with others. But you are doing this for you. As you are exposed to new information, we learn, which causes us to change, which causes us to grow, which could lead to new opportunities. When you say you're willing and able to learn, mean it. Look for those opportunities for self-improvement.

✤ Find Time To Play – No, not sit there and watch TV but to play. Solve a crossword puzzle, exercise, play a pick-up game, go fishing, go knock down a few pins bowling, hit a bucket of balls, take a few hacks in the batting cage, knit, play cards, a board game, bounce a ball, blow bubbles, fly a kite. You need time to recharge, to let your body relax and laugh, to move around and feel alive.

✤ Helping Others, The Value of Volunteering – You read about this earlier. When you give, you show you care; care about making your community a better place. It provides an opportunity to gain experience in a new field. And it makes us feel good inside. This is truly a win-win experience.

CONGRATULATIONS!

By writing down goals, putting measurable expectations by them, executing your plan, and being flexible enough to change them as you see the results, you did it! Keep on doing what successful people do, like writing down goals, and you can achieve your dreams.

About The Author

Frank J. Giudice is a graduate of Gannon University and has been teaching a variety of subjects for over 20 years. He is a certified Social Studies Teacher, Microsoft Office Master Instructor, taught Job Readiness Skills and currently teaches GED classes. Frank has taught students from middle school to adult learners in various settings and capacities, both public and private.

www.ingramcontent.com/pod-product-compliance
Lightning Source LLC
Chambersburg PA
CBHW051535170526
45165CB00002B/749